A
Poet
of the
People

GORDON BOSTIC

PRIMIX
PUBLISHING
THE WRITE CHOICE

Primix Publishing
East Brunswick Office Evolution
1 Tower Center Boulevard, Ste 1510
East Brunswick, NJ 08816
www.primixpublishing.com
Phone: 1-800-538-5788

Published by Primix Publishing: 12/06/2024

ISBN: 979-8-88703-404-1(sc)
ISBN: 979-8-88703-405-8(e)

Library of Congress Control Number: 2024917427

I'm a Poet of the People

I'm a poet of the people
Who tells the people's tales
I speak for those who cannot speak
In depth of their details.

I'm a poet of the people
Who knows the people's ways.
Who's had the same experiences
And lived through the same days.

I'm a poet of the people
Who's lived the people's lives.
Who's had the opportunities
And fell for the same lies.

I'm a poet of the people
Who sings the people's songs.
Who knows what all the people know
And suffered the same wrongs.

I'm a poet of the people,
The masses I embrace;
For I have met the challenges
That they've been forced to face.

I'm a poet of the people,
The humble and demure;
For I have known the hopelessness
That they're forced to endure.

I Wander Through the Monuments

I wander through the monuments
That mark mankind's demise.
I'm saddened by what I see, but
Not totally surprised.

We've teetered on the brink of this
For much too long a time.
Ignorant to what we've become,
Dismissive of the signs.

We have degraded what we were
In pretense of demand
Of reaching for a higher goal
Than can be reached by man.

All that I see are monuments
Denoting what we were.
A people that forgot their place.
Whose time was but a blur.

There May Still Be Avenues

I have lost all my faith in you
But yet, I still implore,
That there may still be avenues
Left for you to explore.

I am certain that you need help,
The way you wear your pain.
But I cannot be here for you,
Just to be used again.

I have offered to get you help,
But you've always refused.
I can't believe that you can't see
That you have all to lose.

I am afraid someday I'll find
You lifeless on the floor.
A victim of the poison that
You refuse to ignore.

The Devil Has Betrayed Us

The Devil has betrayed us
Time and time again
And yet we will turn to him
When we're at wit's end.

We will willing sell our souls
For what's most desired;
No matter the consequence
Or payment required.

We're so shallow and naive
To think we deserve
Anything we think we're owed
By act, deed, or word.

We will gladly prostitute
Just to get ahead
And not waste time worrying
Our fate when we're dead.

Mankind's Broken Dreams

I've wandered through the wasteland
Of mankind's broken dreams
Imagining the horror
And shrinking from the screams.

Mankind dreamed of a paradise
He would not willing earn.
Relying on some magic force
To do its thing in turn.

There's nothing ventured, nothing gained,
For those who have no will.
And yet the dreams may still persist;
They are so hard to kill.

What once was very lush and green
Has now been laid to waste.
A wasteland that's been left behind
To symbolize our fate.

I Have a Soul I Thought Was Lost

I have a soul I thought was lost
To feelings I thought dead;
But when I thought I could not love
Your vision filled my head.

I found you on a winter's break,
Desperate to believe,
That someone who's so beautiful
Could ever notice me.

You began to rule my dreams as
Nightmares beyond control.
Until the point I was obsessed
No matter what the toll.

I was smitten by someone that
I thought I'd never know,
But found your face had haunted me
In ways I could not show.

So I studied all that I could
Of what comprised your days;
So that I could get close to you
By knowing all your ways.

I thought if I could prove to you,
How true to you I'd be;
That maybe you'd give me the chance
To be the one you'd see.

But in the end, I always knew
How hopeless it would be.
That someone who's so beautiful
Would ever notice me.

The Only Joy

I do not have the heart to say
That what we had is done.
But I am sure you've seen the same
As has everyone.

There is no joy in what we have,
Only sorrow and pain.
For when they took our son from us,
Living was not the same.

I do not have the words you need,
Nor sympathy to give.
The only joy we had in life
Was in the way he lived.

I take no joy in saying this
But what we had is gone.
I can't recover from the pain
If you cannot move on.

There are no answers to be gleaned
From all that we've been through.
First to lose my only son and
Then know I'm losing you.

If you're unable to move on,
That's something I need know.
For I have to be done with this
To have another son.

From Love I Abstain

I have often thought of love
But love is not for me.
I do not want the burdens
That love can place on me.

I want to live my life free
Without drama and pain.
I don't want complications
So from love I refrain.

I cherish what I do have.
I've nothing else to gain.
I want an unfettered life
So from love I abstain.

What the Other Sees

You've always meant the world to me
But now that time is gone,
I've met someone that meets my needs
As you have never done.

She looks at me without disdain
And says that I have worth,
Unlike the posture you profess
By treating me like dirt.

She's happy with the way I am
And will not make me change,
Unlike demands that you have made
Where nothing is the same.

Maybe if you had made the time
To see what's there in me,
Then I would not be leaving you
For what the other sees.

I Only Want To Be With You

Whatever worries you've withheld
Are still yours to reclaim.
I only want to be with you
To soothe and ease your pain.

Whatever dreads you have denied
But seem to haunt you still.
I only want to be with you
To make those dreads less real.

Whatever hurt you have endured
That cause your tears to flow.
I only want to be with you
And share the wounds you show.

Whatever fears have haunted you
That serve to feed your fright.
I only want to be with you
And hold you through the night.

I Don't Know What to Make of You

I don't know what to make of you,
So lovely and sublime,
Someone who is so beautiful,
You'll stand the test of time.

I don't know what to make of you,
So tempered and demure,
Who radiates with warmth and love
And tenderness inferred.

I don't know what to make of you,
So sweet and innocent,
As vibrant as a fresh spring day
And pure as heaven sent.

I don't know what to make of you,
Or what was on your mind,
That you would fall in love with me
Is proof you are Divine.

I Dream the Dream No More

When all is hopeless and I'm lost
To know what's next in store.
I know the end is drawing near.
I dream the dream no more.

When expenses have not been met
And no one lives next door.
Life's a struggle I can't endure.
I dream the dream no more.

When loneliness is all I have
With nothing to explore.
I know that hope is all but lost.
I dream the dream no more.

I know my future's an abyss
And failure I implore.
Life is but a bitter pill, so
I dream the dream no more.

The Whispers

The whispers that I hear at night
Consume my heart with dread,
For fear the whispers that I hear
Are whispers of the dead.

The whispers seem to call to me
With passion and desire,
Imploring me to come to them
And lead them from the fire.

The whispers seem to cry for me,
So lost in their despair,
But I'm afraid to answer them
Or let them know I'm there.

The whispers seem to plead with me,
In anguish and in pain,
For all too soon my whispers too,
Are all that will remain.

As Long as You Believe

For all that I have asked of you,
You tried to make me proud
And show yourself to be much more
Than someone in the crowd.

You've never flinched from what I've asked
And tried to do much more.
That's why it's so hard to accept
What fate had held in store.

My dreams replay what my eyes saw
And I'll not soon forget.
I saw my player on the ground,
Not knowing what that meant.

I pray that you will walk someday,
From injury received,
And Hope will be your guardian
As long as we believe.

The Evil That My Father Did

The facts of this came late to me
But I can't bear the shame.
The evil that my father did
Is not my fault or blame.

I can't be held responsible
For what I did not do.
The evil that my father did
Is not what I would do.

I am an individual
Whose actions I will own.
Responsible for my mistakes,
But not what is home grown.

My father was an evil man,
And yes, I am his son.
But person born of principle
That evil has not won.

It's true I am my father's son
But not his protégé.
I will live with my mistakes
But not the ones he made.

She Is Still a Part of Me

When my wife was doomed to die
I thought that I'd die too.
Until I came to realize
That through me she lived too.

She will always be part of me,
As she has always been.
As long as I can still draw breath
She'll be here 'til my end.

It is my way to honor her
And spread her memory.
Although she is no longer here,
She's still a part of me.

I Wander Through the Alleyways

I wander through the alleyways
The dead are apt to roam.
A loser in life's lottery,
With neither hope nor home.

Compassion's not afforded me,
That's why I am alone.
As if I were a criminal
With crimes I must atone.

There is no one to walk with me
Nor offer helping hand.
In fact, the way they stare at me,
You'd think I'm not a man.

I'll wander through the alleyways
Until I face my end.
A beggar to the populace
With no one to call friend.

I Wish I Could Atone

There's nothing that's prescribed for me.
My fate's already sealed.
I know that death's awaiting me
And fear it's all too real.

But in the time that I have left
I wish I could atone,
For all the errors I have made
In workplace and at home.

When forever's our stated goal
We do such stupid things.
With no regard for whom we hurt
Or what our meanness brings.

We always feel we have the time
To make our errors right,
Until we find it's come the time
To face the endless night.

The Lights

I envy those who've seen the light.
A light I have not seen.
Derived by those from other worlds
Who will remain unseen.

What purpose now has brought them here,
Is not for me to say.
I will rely on ignorance
And stay out of their way.

I only fear what schemes they plan.
They live in secrecy.
Just waiting for the perfect time
To test what we believe.

But when it comes to seeing lights,
(The lights I did not see).
Maybe if I avoid the lights
The lights won't look for me.

I Don't Know Where the Danger Lies

I don't know where the danger lies,
But know it lies in wait.
In patience it will bide its time
To pounce on my mistakes.

I don't know where the danger hides,
Keeping just out of sight;
Just crouching in its hiding place
Hoping that I'll take flight.

I don't know where the danger lies
But know it waits for me.
For soon enough the danger wins
And from life I'll be freed.

I Live To Be a Champion

I live to be a champion
And bask in the acclaim;
To live as a celebrity
And reach the Hall of Fame.

I live to be a champion
And rich beyond my dreams;
To be the one who's most admired
And know what famous means.

I live to be a champion
And envy of my peers;
To be the one reporters seek
And never hear the jeers.

I live to be a champion
And bask in the applause;
To know the fame that legends know
And leader of a cause.

I live to be a champion
But know I'll never be;
For all the talent that's required
Was not given to me.

Love Lost in the Night

Sometimes when I am all alone,
And lost in my despair,
I wonder what became of us,
And if you even care.

I've lived a life of solitude,
Too proud to dare admit,
I wished to be your shining knight
And found I was not it.

I loved too much to know I failed
But failure was my plight.
And loneliness is my reward
For love lost in the night.

For All My Friends

For all my friends that've come and gone,
Some whom I barely knew,
I wish I could express my love
For what I put you through.

You gave me strength when I was down,
And tried to show the way.
I could arise from tragedy
And face a brand-new day.

You gave me purpose when I'd none
And took me by the hand
To lead me from the darkness that
I thought fated to land.

You gave me hope when I had none
And showed me love again.
You were there when I needed you,
To prove yourself my friend.

I Hear Your Voice

I hear your voice calling to me,
From somewhere in the night,
Imploring for my quick return
And rescue from my plight.

I hear your voice pleading for me,
From somewhere in the dark,
In prayer for my safe return
From what keeps us apart.

I hear your voice sobbing for me
Beyond the battlefield,
In agony that I'll be felled
And to death slowly yield.

I hear your voice so dimly now
As my life comes to end,
And now I know I won't return
To see my wife and friends.

Feelings

I do not deal with feelings
For feelings often lie.
Feelings tend to interfere
With how we live our lives.

I've grown to fear the feelings
For feelings can deceive.
They led me to wrongly think
What I deeply believed.

I hate that I have feelings,
That force me to recall,
Memories of you and I
That came before the fall.

I do not feel the feelings
The pain's too great to bear.
I don't like the way I feel
In knowing you're not there.

Life Is Not a Sprint

Life is not a sprinter's dream
But more a marathon.
Where pace is almost paramount
If journey's to be won.

Whatever life has planned for us,
It's not for us to see.
Life is about experience
And not what we believe.

We hope to find fortune and fame,
But so few of us do.
We're captives of the here and now,
And what we must live through.

For life's a journey hard to meet,
With dreams we cannot find.
Life is more than mortality;
It is a state of mind.

To Be a Better Being

Some say that we're reborn each day
To live our lives anew
With chances to correct mistakes
Or actions to undo.

We have a chance to recreate
The profiles we employ
And take the time to sprinkle in
A little bit of joy.

Each day presents another chance
For us to make amends
And hook up with old enemies
Who now could be our friends.

'Cause with the rising of the sun
Our slates can be wiped clean
Presenting opportunity
To be a better being.

I Swim the Shadows of Despair

I swim the shadows of despair,
Unfeeling and unmoved.
A creature who avoids the light
Because the darkness soothes.

I sail the oceans of despair
In vessel full of holes.
As someone who's been cast aside
And never will be whole.

I sink within pools of despair
My struggles soon to end.
Drowning from a love lost
Before it could begin.

Expectations

We walk through life pretending
We are not who we are.
Delusional in thinking
We're born to be a star.

We're born with expectations
Of what our life should mean.
Never understanding that
Life is a surreal dream.

We are born to a blank slate
Of where our lives may lead.
God has given us the choice
If only we believed.

Expectations weigh on us
To be what we can't be.
For no one will take the time
To stop and really see.

We're born as individuals
With goals we wish to claim,
But fall short of expectations
With no one we can blame.

Dancing with the Devil

If you dance with the Devil
You will be burned by fire.
For the Devil has no friends
Unless they feed his ire.

The Devil is pure evil
And the bane of our time.
For he's become part of us
And settled in our minds.

The evil we've come to fear
Comes by another name.
For the Devil has our soul
Because we play his game.

I Dream That Dream No More

Despite whatever I have dreamed,
I dream that dream no more.
I have lost all I ever dreamed
When you walked out the door.

I had visions of picket fence
And lawn, so lush and green.
But these were not the things you wished.
You longed for bigger dreams.

So my dreams have withered and died,
As most dreams tend to do;
And I will never dream again
For my great dream was you.

Your Regrets

I'll no longer accept regrets
For which you seem imbibe.
I have a life I wish to live
And I'll not be denied.

I wasted faith and trust in you,
For you live to deceive.
For once I pledged my love to you
And heartbreak I received.

You promised to be true to me,
An oath you have forsworn,
But now excuses tend to mount
With patience quickly worn.

You've proved that trust is lost on you,
For trust you do not know,
And love is much a mystery
You don't know how to show.

How meaningless are your regrets
As you will never see,
That I was always true to you,
And you will never be.

I Lost What Made Me, Me

Somewhere in the life I've lived
I lost what made me, me.
A sense of worth that I enjoyed
Which I no longer see.

I lost the promise I once held
To live a life alone;
As someone took my heart away
With light that I once owned.

I only loved once in my life,
A love that's now denied.
The love I thought that we still shared,
Until you said "Good-bye."

I lost whatever I once was
With slamming of the door.
A journey out of excellence
To be that me, no more.

Maybe

Maybe another time and place
We could be more than friends.
Maybe our passives would run loose
And find where they may end.

Maybe if we were given time
Our love could somehow bloom.
Maybe if no one interfered
Our love wouldn't end too soon.

Maybe if we are left alone
We'd have the chance to find
If we're truly compatible
Or simply to love blind.

Maybe if we are left to find
We all are God's lament
For He sprinkled his love on us…
A love we have not spent.

The Land of Long-Lost Souls

I've seen the land of long-lost souls
Where dreams have come to die.
Where all that mankind dared to hope
Was proved to be a lie.

I've seen the struggles and the sins
That keep mankind at bay;
With nothing much to comfort him
That will not block his way.

This land is always occupied
For dreams so quickly die.
Then dragging down the withered souls
Who will never know why.

The Paradox

Life is too much a paradox
For what we have achieved.
When we think that we have found truth.
We find what we don't need.

We are the victims of our past,
And sins we must confess
For what our lives have brought to us
Is nothing more than mess.

We rely on the things we know,
And we don't know that much.
All the things we think we know, shows
We're really out of touch.

So all that we have built and done
May soon be swept away
By someone who will not fall for
The paradox malaise.

All the Time

All the transgressions we've endured,
That make it hard to live,
Are multiplied by simple fact
That we cannot forgive.

We waste our time pursuing things
We truly do not need,
And sacrifice for what we want,
The values we believe.

We squander opportunities
That are so hard to find
For lack of effort we expend
Thinking we're saving time.

But in the end, the shortcuts fail
To give us peace of mind,
In the pursuit of answers which
Elude us all the time.

Just Tell Me What I Need to Know

I hate people who are verbose
With what they have to say.
Just tell me what I need to know
And I'll be on my way.

Like politicians who are thrilled
With sounds of their own voice.
Just tell me what I need to know
So I know I have choice.

I am weary of listening
To those who have no clue.
Just tell me what I need to know
Before I'm done with you.

If You're to Play for Me

I must demand commitment
If you're to play for me,
And I'll accept nothing less
If you're to play for me.

I must demand your respect,
If you're to play for me;
And a resolve to be proved
If you're to play for me.

I must demand attention
If you're to play for me,
Details are of great import
If you're to play for me.

I must demand your loyalty
If you're to play for me;
Your belief in what I teach
So champions we'll be.

I Was a Legend

I was a legend in my time,
But my time's come and gone.
Its time that someone new emerged.
Someone to carry on.

I was the face of victory
That no one could ignore;
But now I'm lost to history
That no one will restore.

There's no one to remember me
For I am lost in time.
I'm someone from the long-lost past
Whose name won't come to mind.

I'm a Poet of the People

I'm a poet of the people
For I know the people's ways.
I know what they endure at night
And what consumes their days.

I'm a poet of the people
For I've seen what they've seen.
I know the things the people know
And I've been where they've been.

I'm a poet of the people
Who's known the people's woes.
Who has faced the people's failures
And knows what people know.

I'm a poet of the people
Whose drama I have lived.
Who has faced the people's trauma
With nothing left to give.

I'm a poet of the people
Who's known the same disgrace.
Who knows what it means to rise with
Another day to face.

Those Days of Yore

I hunger for those days of yore
When worries, I had none.
When I'd deem to call it a night
With rising of the sun.
But now I am asleep by nine
And up before the sun;
With worries I seem accumulate
As does most anyone.

I yearn to live those days of yore
When life was fast and free.
With no one I must answer to
And no one controlled me.
But now I follow a schedule
To which I must adhere.
A time and place for ev'rything
To make sure my mind's clear.

I dream about those days of yore
When you were at my side,
And we would spend those carefree days
In love we could not hide.
But now I spend my days alone
And nights in solitude.
For I no longer have my youth
And you're denied me too.

Images Will Last

I must approach the future
As I've approached the past.
Whatever good I think I've done,
I know will never last.

My failures serve to burden me
As anchors to my past.
Whatever good I tried to do
I know will never last.

Whatever people think of me,
Concerning what's my past,
Images are what stay with them,
For images will last.

The Great "Why"

I walk amid the battlefield
Where my friends lived and died;
And wonder the accomplishment
That made so many cry.

What evil purpose did we thwart
Requiring my friends die?
What rationale did we present
To answer the great "why."

All I see are ashes now, from
Carnage that we have wrought
And question what it is we won
That all these lives have bought.

Tolerance

I won't live a life of tolerance
For some things are just wrong.
And there are those who know it's true
But will not sing the song.

We use the term of tolerance
To mask what is untrue.
To influence that we accept
What others want to do.

Whenever they want nature changed
Its tolerance they cry;
To keep in secret their designs
So not to be denied.

For those who are intolerant
Are the first ones to say,
That we're the ones intolerant,
To keep them from their way.

Perfection's Hard to Find

Perfection can be hard to find
Depending on the view.
There's nothing perfect in this world
Regardless of the view.

Perfection is a fancy term
That's mostly used for art.
For perfect love can never be,
Just count the broken hearts.

So when perfection can't be found,
Look for the next best thing,
Remembering your telephone
And giving me a ring.

Whenever You Have Need of Me

Whenever you have need of me
You merely have to call.
No matter what business I have,
You know I'll drop it all.

Whatever you may need of me
You merely have to ask.
For I will give you anything
And in the giving, bask.

Wherever you may need me be
You merely have to point.
For you know I will be there so
As not to disappoint.

For I am so in love with you
Your bidding I will do.
As you have claimed my heart and soul
And my devotion too.

The Graveyard

I meander through the graveyard
Of those who came before,
To wonder what the stories were
And what their lives were for.

Did they live lives of happiness
Or struggled to get by?
Did they receive the fruits of life
Or did they simply die?

Were they trying to just survive
Or were they of some means?
Had their lives become meaningless
Or only how it seems?

The questions seem to bother me
More than they truly should.
For soon I may be resting here
As I had feared I would.

Horror

There is no way I can transcribe
The horror that I feel,
To know I've seen my greatest fears
And know that they are real.

There is no way I can describe
The terror that takes hold
When face-to-face with what you fear
And feel your blood run cold.

There's no way I can understand
How such horror can live,
But horror does exist in life
And it does not forgive.

The Urge

I struggle through the undergrowth
Of my basic desires
Unwilling to make compromise
Or quench the raging fire.

I am lost to my passion's throes
Unable to control
The urges that come over me
And make my juices roll.

So I stalk the dank alleyways
In search of brand-new prey
And introduce myself to them
On this, their final day.

I only kill because I must
In answer to the urge
Until they come to track me down
And from this world be purged.

The Will to Trust

I hate to be the bearer,
But bad news travels fast.
Sometimes secrets will escape,
For secrets do not last.

We fill our lives with secrets
In hopes that no one knows,
What we fear and what we love,
We try to never show.

As long as we keep secrets
Our lives are incomplete.
It means we don't dare to trust
So secrets we must keep.

We have too many secrets
For truth has been denied.
We have lost the will to trust
Because we never tried.

I Dream the Dreams

I dream the dreams that dreamers dream
When dreamers dare to dream;
And look for things as yet unknown
That no one else has seen.

I walk the path no other walks
But do so with disdain.
For no one else will walk the path
In fear they will find shame.

I say the words no one will speak
For they are too afraid
Of drawing ire from media
Who've clearly lost their way.

I think the thoughts no other thinks,
For fear they may be wrong,
And dare to challenge all I know
In picture, word or song.

Advances in Technology

Advances in technology
Have born a heavy cost.
To which we are oblivious
To see what we have lost.

We've lost what was humanity,
Despite what we believe.
Technology consumes our lives
So much so we should grieve.

We can no longer interact
As people once enjoyed.
We're caught up in technology
And it's what we employ.

Conversation is lost to us
For texting's what we know.
And passions that we once displayed
We fear to ever show.

Growing into automatons
That have no heart or soul
Just creatures of technology
Who have no other role.

We Keep Too Many Secrets

We have kept so many secrets
To hide who we've become.
We've lost our own identities
And could be anyone.

We cover up who we may be
As if we were ashamed
Of the person we've grown to be
By any other name.

We fall to judgments others make
And let those judgments rule.
We see ourselves through others' eyes
So needful to be cool.

We keep all too many secrets,
So no one else can see
The greatness that we keep inside,
Afraid that we'll set free

That to Which We're Bound

All the tests that we've undergone
Have led us to this place,
Where mortality is something
That we are forced to face.

We have done our best to survive
The perils of our time,
In hopes that our posterity
Can see we're in decline.

We hope that we have left this world
Much better than we found,
So our children have better lives
Than that to which we're bound.

A Path to Glory

There is a path to glory
If only we'd believe
That what we have to offer
Is more than we receive.

There is a day of glory
That's not beyond our reach
If only we'd the courage
To practice what we preach.

There is no silver lining
If we will not extend
The prospect of forgiving
To families and friends.

There can be no hopelessness
As long as we believe,
The answers lie within us
To only be perceived.

Stuck in an Abyss

I have no desire to listen
To all of your complaints.
I know I'm not the perfect man
And, clearly, not a saint.

But I am not the total fool
That you surely believe.
I am more the every man
Who has his basic needs.

You spend your days ignoring me,
Denying me at night,
And anything I dare to say
Is fodder for a fight.

I do not know where my love went
But she lives here no more.
The woman who captured my heart
Has long walked out the door.

And now I'm stuck in an abyss
With one who loves no more.
A bitch who thinks she is too good
To live with one deplored.

I Live a Life Invisible

I live a life invisible
So no one else can see,
That I am much more fallible
Than I should truly be.

I try slip under the radar
So no one else will know,
The anguish that consumes my heart
That never seems let go.

I try to evade the limelight
So no one knows my dreams,
The wishes that I hope come true
No matter what that means.

I try to meld into the crowd
So no one there can spy,
How close I am to breaking down
As life slowly slips by.

I live a life invisible
So no one can get close
And steal from me the deep desires
That I covet the most.

I Was Not the Teammate

I was never the teammate that
I'd thought that I would be.
Someone who would always support
The player next to me.

But I allowed my vanity
To overcome desire.
I found I was not the teammate
To which I had aspired.

Whenever ego takes control,
We try to do too much,
And in the effort doom our team
By betraying, their trust.

Memories

There's no refuge from memories,
For from them we can't hide.
Memories are forever ours;
The good ones and the lies.

Memories will remain with us
As long as we still breathe.
Sometimes to fight the loneliness
Sometimes to fill a need.

Some memories we can't forget,
And fear we never can.
Because the pain that we recall
Is something we can't stand.

The Task

The dead bodies that I still see
Littered across the plain.
Of those who'd lived and bravely died,
But bravely died in vain.

They threw themselves into the fray
Without any regard
To the danger we'd present to
Repel their reckless charge.

They surged at us, wave after wave,
And wave by wave, they fell.
Men who died so honorably
We swore to tell their tale.

But in the end, when it was through,
And none of them still lived.
We admired the gallantry
And what they'd willing give.

The sacrifice that they had made
Was more than should be asked.
They were ordered to fight and die
And they took on the task.

I Don't Believe

I don't believe in musing
About what should have been.
Whatever's meant to happen
Will work out in the end.

I don't believe in stewing
About my lot in life.
I've learned to accept my fate
And live beyond the strife.

I don't believe regretting
The things I have not done.
For I did the things I could
And that's a battle won.

I don't believe bemoaning
The things I never had.
Instead I like to celebrate
The things that make me glad.

Until My Journey Is Complete

I hear the wind whisper to me
I live life way too hard.
Too many risks I willing take
And safety, disregard.

It seems I've always wished for death
To tempt fate as I do.
Whether it's by reckless choice or
I do not think things through.

I've cheated death so many times
I know the odds are good,
If I continue this reckless path
I'll meet the fate I should.

But change is not an easy thing,
Nor something I can do.
Until my journey is complete,
I'll have to see it through.

As We're Reduced to Tears

We are a land divided
Because we have been played
By shady politicians
Who have a life that's made.

They penalize the populace
So they can live as kings.
And work to regulate the lives
Of all their subject beings.

They live a life of opulence
At all of our expense.
Thinking that they were born to rule
An ignorant populace.

They come to rule in poverty;
Retired as millionaires.
Regaling us with verbiage that
They think will make us care.

There're devious in their purpose
With such an evil plan.
A plan that is to divide us
So they are in demand.

We are made a land divided
Because they wish it so
They thrive on the divisiveness
That helps their power grow.

I Look to Cast My Future

I look to cast my future
As stones upon the sea,
To see where the ripples run
And what they say to me.

Concentric rings as they spread,
I watch the ripples grow.
Having faith the ripples point
Direction I should go.

In the end the ripples fade
And answers still elude.
With future still enigma
My destiny holds true.

I Only Wish to Be With You

I only wish to be with you
And hold you through the night.
To lay myself down next to you
And stay 'til morning's light.

I only wish to be with you
And hold you close to me.
To know the warmth that you exude
That washes over me.

I only wish to be with you
And know the love we share.
To know the touch you willing give
To let me know you care.

I only wish to be with you
And know the love you own.
To pledge my life and love to you
With promise of a home.

If Love Truly Was Your Goal

I must take my leave of you
For I do not believe
There's a future we can share,
For you live to deceive.

You've lied to me more than once
And laughed, that I'm a fool.
I will not be used by you,
Nor will I be your tool.

If love truly was your goal
I'd say I was surprised,
For all I've seen of your love
Is little more than lies.

Sometimes We Must Forgive

There are times injustice rules
And pain we must relive.
To find the strength to move on
Sometimes we must forgive.

Life is fraught with highs and lows
And that's the way we live.
To face failures we've incurred,
Sometimes we must forgive.

There are those who'll spit on us
For spite is what they give,
And we face dilemma that
Sometimes we must forgive.

We reflect on our mistakes,
Mistakes we've tried outlive;
And to keep them in our past,
Sometimes we must forgive.

Promises You'll Never Keep

I marvel at the mastery
In which you play the field.
Not looking for relationships
Nor caring how they feel.

You spend your life in one night stands
For comfort in the night.
Then off to find another love
Before the evening's lights.

You are a slave to your desires,
Amoral in belief,
In how you woo the willing ones
For personal relief.

It's obvious you know no shame
Nor love can you conceive.
You are devoid of tenderness
You're willing to receive.

Your life is but an endless loop,
Hopping from bed to bed;
With promises you'll never keep,
Until you're cold and dead.

I Am Not a Living Legend

I am not a living legend,
But one who tried too hard.
A man who gave his heart and soul
Without his own regard.

I have lived through the leanest times
Hoping for a reprieve,
That someone in their ignorance
Would somehow just believe.

That failure's not an option and
Surrender is not me.
I am not a living legend
But one day hope to be.

Where Milk and Honey Flows

I want to journey to the land
Where milk and honey flows.
Where pestilence does not exist
And evil does not go.

Where issues of faith are unknown
And truth remains in play.
Where people love in solemn trust
Because that is their way.

Where no one has an enemy
Because hate is unknown,
And hunger is a memory
From seeds carefully sown.

Where everyone lives in peace
And no one is ashamed.
Where all are held responsible
And no one's held to blame.

I want to journey to the land
Where milk and honey flows,
And vanish from the wretched life
That I have come to know.

A Case of Paranoid

I'll have my vengeance, in due time,
For what they've done to me.
By spying on my ev'ry move
And tapping my TV.

They follow me as I sojourn,
And listen to my calls.
I know I cannot be alone
For they have bugged my walls.

Their satellites look down on me,
From way beyond my sight.
And I know they have searched my house
When I'm asleep at night.

The doctors think I may be ill,
But how can I be sure?
For how can I be confident
That they don't want me cured?

The Man could have persuaded them,
To try put me away.
So I'd no longer be a threat
Their secrets to be saved.

The doctors say they're tired of me,
But I think they're annoyed.
For they think I may suffer from
A case of paranoid.

Dreams

Dreams are not meant to be kept
For dreams are made to share.
They show us new directions
Of which we're unaware.

Dreams portend who we may be
How high we can aspire.
They can reveal out true selves
And serve as to inspire.

Dreams can make us persevere
When all around us fails.
Dreams can be our last refuge
Before the last ship sails.

Willing Paid the Price

There's nothing good that has been gained
Without some sacrifice.
For nothing in this life is free,
There always is a price.

Whatever goal we wish achieve
There will be sacrifice,
If we're to know the joy that comes
From having paid the price.

Too many choose avoid the risk
Or fear to take a chance,
For failure may be consequence
And they won't dance that dance.

There's nothing good that has been gained
Without the sacrifice
That man has been willing to make
And willing paid the price.

You Are My Coach

You are my coach and I will do
Whatever's asked of me,
And I will dedicate myself
To be what I should be.

I only ask that you be kind
In what you have to say,
And know that I will make mistakes
For that's the game we play.

I train as hard as I know how
And give practice my all.
But fear if I make a mistake
My name you'll scream and call.

I am but putty in your hands
With promise I will grow,
But only if you're patient with
The promise that I show.

Applaud the effort that I give.
Mistakes you must excuse.
But I will not be subject to
Constant verbal abuse.

I Have Been the Butt of Jokes

I have been the butt of jokes
Because I'm not well liked.
I have known what outcasts know
Because that is my life.

I don't know what others know
As how they can fit in.
But it's much harder for me
Because I have no friends.

I possess no social grace
Nor friendly attitude.
I live a life of loneliness
Bounded by solitude.

I've often thought they'd know my name
If I would choose to rule,
And arm myself beyond belief
Before I went to school.

And with the last breath that I draw,
After they gun me down;
I wonder if they'll know my name
For what I'll be renown.

My Mind Is Mirror to the World

My mind is mirror to the world
Of all I did not know
And sees the possibilities
The world is apt to show.

My mind is mirror to the world
And will enlighten me
For there is much more to this world
Than I ever believed.

My mind is mirror to the world
Reflecting what I've seen.
The magic that is nature's way.
The way it's always been.

Where, Oh Where

Where, oh where, does my love hide,
That she is kept from me?
When all that I've ever felt
Is what she means to me.

Where, oh where, is my love kept,
That she can't come to me?
When all that I've ever wished
Is have her close to me.

Where, oh where, is my love jailed,
That she cannot be free?
When all that I need to do
Is have her next to me.

Where, oh where, is my love held,
That she can't run to me;
Or was she a volunteer
To say she's done with me?

A Sense of Urgency

I feel your sense of urgency
Because we do not win;
But we do not work hard enough
To see our failures end.

There is no glory in defeat,
Even when we play well.
We've started to believe the myth
That we're under a spell.

But, truth be told, we do not try
To be the best we could.
We don't expend the energy
We know we really should.

So our failures begin to mount
As losing we accept,
For we will not work hard enough
To earn our own respect.

My Life's Not Theirs to Live

I do not care what others think
My life's not theirs to live.
I strive to leave a legacy
That I will not outlive.

I do not walk in others' steps
The steps I take are mine.
I live for my accomplishments
In body, soul, and mind.

I do not live for their critiques
I judge myself too hard.
And in final analysis
I try to live too large.

And yet, I hope, the effort made
Will never be ignored.
I've tried to do the best I could
With all I could employ.

A Public Service

A public service murder
Is one that is deserved.
Someone justice cannot touch
But to whom justice's served.

There are those who can't be touched
By long arm of the law.
So public service must be dealt
When justice tends to fall.

Although it is not allowed
Public service's become
The last vessel of justice
When justice must be won.

Only They Would Win

I pray to God that I am wrong,
But know I've been betrayed
By those I hold responsible
For the mistakes I've made.

I was misguided and maligned
By those I trusted most.
And they're the ones that chastised me
For giving up the ghost.

In truth, I never had a chance,
For fate was cruel to me;
As those in whom I placed my trust
Too quickly turned on me.

So I was left to hold the bag,
As I was meant to do.
They live a life of luxury
I was not privy to.

Now I know that I was not wrong,
In ever trusting them.
They sang a song of confidence
That only they would win.

I Need to Know What You Know

I need to know all you dream
And wish for secretly.
So I can then mold myself
To one you'd wish to see.

I have watched you from afar
Too shy to dare approach;
For fear that any advance
Would lead to your reproach.

I have lived and dreamed of you
For way too many days,
But I've seen how many beaus
Have wooed you with their praise.

If I'm to find my inroads,
And try to catch your eye.
I need to know what you know
To give it my best try.

I've Never Been the Danger

I've never been the danger
You've made me out to be.
I know I have a temper,
And that's not lost on me.

But you, I have never harmed,
Nor threaten to do so.
As angry as I've become
With what you think you know.

You're so sure that you know me,
You have to dig and pick;
Driving me into a rage
That escalates real quick.

You work too hard to flaunt my flaws
And never see the good;
And never, ever gave a thought
To aid me as you should.

I've never been the problem.
The problem lies with you.
Goading me to do the things
I normally wouldn't do.

I Watched My Cat Die

I sadly watched as my cat died
But not from my neglect.
She was a victim of disease
The vet did not detect.

I had to watch her waste away,
Though loving 'til the end.
It was hard to watch her passing
For she was more than friend.

We treat our pets as family,
In all too many ways.
Maybe because, it is the love,
That brightens up our days.

That's why their passing is so hard,
To have their love denied.
For what we have as family
Is people who won't try.

I'm a Poet of the People

I'm a poet of the people
Who knows where he belongs.
A hidden member of the crowd
Who tries to get along.

I'm a poet of the people
Who has seen what they see.
Betrayed by high echelon
And loss of dignity.

I'm a poet of the people
Who knows the people's joys.
Who's been behind the cameras
And seen why they're annoyed.

I'm a poet of the people
Who's had bad days and good,
But always strives to live a life
In manner as he should.

I'm a poet of the people
For that is what I am.
For I have lived the people's life
And done the best I can.

About the Author

Gordon Bostic was born in West Virginia and grew up in Virginia. A graduate of James Madison University and Fairleigh Dickinson University, he worked as a computer scientist and a software engineer for most of his life. Gordon began writing at a young age as a way of expressing his feelings and his view of the world. He has an interest in telling his stories to people in one way or another. *A Poet of the People* is his first book of poetry. Gordon currently lives on the Jersey Shore with his wife, Susan.